YOU CAN BE THE CREAM THAT RISES IN A DOWN-TRENDING ECONOMY

YOU CAN BE THE CREAM THAT RISES IN A DOWN-TRENDING ECONOMY

ANTONETH L. WILLIAMS

YOU CAN BE THE CREAM THAT RISES IN A DOWN-TRENDING ECONOMY

iUniverse books may be ordered through booksellers or by contacting:

iUniverse
1663 Liberty Drive
Bloomington, IN 47403
www.iuniverse.com
1-800-Authors (1-800-288-4677)

ISBN: 978-1-4620-6849-4 (sc)
ISBN: 978-1-4620-6850-0 (e)

Print information available on the last page.

iUniverse rev. date: 02/23/2016

CONTENTS

CONTENTS

INTRODUCTION

THE CREAM RISES TO THE TOP=
'SURVIVAL OF THE FITTEST"

William Faulkner, upon receiving the Nobel Prize for Literature at City Hall, New York, 1949, said, "I believe that man will not merely endure. He will prevail. He is immortal, not because he alone among creatures has an inexhaustible voice, but because he has a soul, a spirit capable of compassion, sacrifice and endurance." This is a powerful connotation to **introduce the "enigma" THE CREAM RISES TO THE TOP - portraying that a self-motivated person will rise above the complexities of life. The Cream rising to the top is a natural and irreversible phenomenon in every possible situation and even in times like these that try the soul!**

WHEN is the last time you felt on top of the world? What was the occasion? Had you just launch a new job, finally finished a challenging project or experience some other kind of success? **Opportunities or success as we know** it, are not easy to embrace today without **positive, objective determination**. It is said "The future is not a gift, it's an attainment." True! However, we find ourselves now living in a nation that's depressed and feeling enslaved by a huge national debt and pernicious unemployment. Yes, **WE ARE THERE!** Reflexive reaction is often irrational so the government is still trying to figure out who "owns" the problems while people in America are held in custodial depression for lack of constructive, decisive, and effective legal policies to be administrated by the Federal government. They need to find rational response, by utilizing the input of

Antoneth L. Williams

heads of States and municipalities who are closely aligned to the situations in communities of people suffering from the maladies of depression.

IT is difficult to do an analysis of cause and effect, nor is it worth positive energy to understand all the negative impositions that have exasperated people today. There is no normalcy or impending trends that can bring a sense of relief unless you look for it within yourself and come up with solutions that will create a win-win situation. This is when the CREAM must rise with determination to find and utilize rational responses to the questions. **I know that this too will pass.** Dreams do not have an expiration date, and **Opportunity is never lost. You can create them.**

THE ECOMOMIC CLIMATE IMPACTING AMERICA TODAY.

WE are in the middle **of a crisis we did not create**. The economic crises have gone global and most countries including America are not managing the realities of it or show a high capacity for critical adjustments. America is tethering weakly between overreaction and under-reaction, and **"you are there**." But, YOU cannot inject any sense of immediacy into the current events or intervene, personally or intellectually, into the muddle of the different approaches to hasten or to improve the pathetic economic recovery. Today, it seems closer to a full-blown recession.

AND we are reluctantly participating in the issues of a global economic stalemate and at home the growing concerns of raising the "Debt Ceiling". We indeed realize all of the above troubles were inevitable, but not be so intruding. The conflicts and hardships are in our faces. They are pervasive, and the speed of negative changes are rapid, non-discriminating and, the prospect of a more crushing, unprecedented recession looms dark like an approaching storm clouds. **Faith works**! and "**This too will pass**." We all hope that this recession does not become "an ugly race to the bottom." Let us be optimistic despite the deadly drama of it all. We must work hard and smart to be the Cream that will always rise to the top.

UNIQUE PERSPECTIVES ON HOW TO RISE.

THIS book identifies and postulate some ways whereby anyone can achieve full potential to be the CREAM that rises. You must intentionally seek a measure of incremental empowerment and independence first, by updating your knowledge base, and skills in a more expansive way, especially in the new multi-stranded information technologies, (IT), science and web-based communication techniques. Another way to increase your focus on SURVIVAL is by extending in a solid nucleus of like-minded people through networking, job training programs, local technical schools and all other positive methods to obtain those objectives. Attend free seminars, free workshops, work fairs, even local political town hall meetings. None of these is off limits. Wake up your "positive **energy**" to all opportunities!

SURVIVAL IS FOR THE FITTEST **in this** economic Crises**:** **To those of you who are fortunate to** have a job, (full or part-time,) you must intensify your efforts to **survive the new negative feedback frenzies** that are rampant in most of the current downsized workplaces. While you are surviving and responding to a variety of personal needs, to become the CREAM, you will also have to create unique approaches to rising up in the workplace. Through strong focus, skills, experience, talent, and knowledge of information processing, of utilizing updated and higher-level technology gadgets, you can create the job that you want, while improving your knowledge and capabilities. Also include VOLUNTEERING in areas of your job interests, and in some meaningful ways, create a climate of trust. Show up in areas of social services where human needs are more critical. Some jobs openings may become eventual, and positive feedback from volunteering will be essential in getting you jobs in the future.

IN this book, I'll share necessary capabilities and some proven strategies for success: for students, the non/under/unemployed professionals, new employees, blue collars, supervisors and managers. These pointers are vital enhancements if your intention is to be **"the CREAM that will rise and bring others up with you." Also, the** book will help you unlock all your potential and supercharge your motivation to be the **Cream (the best) in** whatever career or occupation you may strive to attain in life. You need to work hard, and smart, to achieve remarkable success whether you work for a corporation in a white collar job or in blue-collar positions in any area of industries. As a great reminder, a **scattering of people today, still** remember the tragic times of the 1930s. Their stories of hardships resonate with today's national and many international news headlines.

YES, we have entered a strategic and compelling era; a new thrust in the loss of livelihood, homesteads, jobs, family ties, financial security, goals and dreams. They are surviving with mayhem, whiplash, and emotional agitation in a neutral economy, that is resisting, or unresponsive to the wide and lengthy intervention of government and private enterprises. It is repulsive to human dignity and have resulted, increasingly, in negative local and world-wide consequences. Survival statistics are growing as people become more dependent on government to provide for their basic needs for food and shelter.

UNIQUE PERSPECTIVES FOR THE CREAM.

Many Americans' dreams have faded. But by an increasingly viable ways and means, leaders from all walks of life today and in other generations, discover the secrets of negotiations and summary compromise that have pushed them to the top of their industry or social movement. They **know "the** future is not a gift, it's an attainment." Winning the future means reinventing ourselves to respond to the new requirements and reforms of this current era of information technology. We have to rise up to the challenges, responsibilities and innovations, and KNOW what is important versus what is imperative, how to balance challenges versus crises, and understand new programs and their purposes.

HOW can you reach full potential? Most people know the realities of an economic stability that has zigzagged and remains in-and-out of reach since the 1980s. **"We are all there" today. Life shrinks or expands in proportion to one's courage.** This book has messages of courage and motivation that will intentionally result in personal achievements encouraging you to rise up as **the CREAM**. This paraphrase is very appropriate for our times: **"We are troubled on every side, yet not distressed; we are perplexed, but not in despair. Persecuted, but not for forsaken; cast down, but not destroyed." 2nd Corinthian 4: 8-9. Have Faith in God! You have to start somewhere to get where you want to be.**

PEOPLE are innately inquisitive creatures. We investigate and explore. Normally, we are continually searching for new experiences, objects and surroundings as life shrinks or expand in proportion to one's courage. When confronted with some new phenomenon or with something inexplicable, we want to understand how it came about, how it works. But, all the knowledge and understanding you have received from sciences and technologies cannot fully explain the current vicious, astronomical, acute complexities of this economic down trend spiraling with no end in sight. Do not let these contingencies weaken your stubborn goodness and, or relentless faith.

IMBEDDED in the matrix of today's crisis, is the gnawing factors in job procurement, retention and advancement, the loss of homesteads, family cohesiveness and stability, depletion of money, and a new populace dependent on entitlement programs and social agencies for daily survival. All these developments provide vital clues to why **YOU**, in essence, "THE CREAM" has nowhere else to go but to rise to the top." THE CREAM, **the guru of the self-help movement,** has strongly influenced generations to develop and incorporate personal growth opportunities, outline strategies and to include them into their everyday lives. Let's be rational, not everyone has the potential, capabilities or motivation to reach the top echelon. If this were possible, all companies, businesses and corporations would have more managers that workers. But those of you with a "positive Energy" should utilize "down" times to promote and escalate your ambitions. The **employment statistics will change in the near future**. Make preparation now for that coming eventuality.

IMPERATIVES for Graduate Students:

I advance here to address all the happy graduating High School and College students and their proud parents. Intriguingly, most students graduating from colleges today are going back to live at home because of outrageous college debts, and that, for most parents, graduation doesn't mark the end of your child's education - it's only the beginning! One memorable song, we've come to associate with most graduation is "Pomp and Circumstance" played all across the country in the spring. "Young people will line up in cap and gown to make that long nervous march to a podium for a very official looking document called a diploma. When the final name is read, and the last sheepskin handed out, someone will announce "Ladies and gentlemen, I present to you the class of—!" "There will be a collective whoop as jubilant graduates jump to their feet and toss their caps high in the air. Dads will beam, Moms will weep. It will be a day to celebrate. But as you know, Mom and Dad, graduation ceremonies do not mark the end of education - it is only the beginning! From now on it will be the critical decade which could **have a major influence** on the decisions they'll be making over the next several years." James Dobson, Focus,1998.

NEW EMPLOYEES - (NEED TO KNOW)

CONGRATULATIONS! And my best wishes to all of you for a prosperous and significant career! **I believe in encouragement**. However, opportunities and JOB success as we knew it once, are not easy to embrace today without your purposive determination. There is so much disappointment all around us to stunt ambitions and defeat our goals that only the CREAM will rise, or the FITTEST WILL SURVIVE. Upon graduating you'll find yourselves living in a nation that's depressed and feel enslaved by a huge local and national debt. **WE ARE THERE!** This book has identify the obstacles that may get in your way of achieving equanimity, or your full potential. You will be tried and tested repeatedly as a job applicant, **but you cannot give up**. That is not a strategy. It took Thomas Edison many failures to create the light bulb. Who would have guessed that civilization could impede positive life strides?

THIS should be the time for you to move from skimming at the shallow edge of entitlement programs, PELL Grants, $50.00 scholarships and odd jobs, to real empowerment and independence? **The federal government does not want you on their payroll. They want you to pay to them income taxes, and every other conceivable tax you can think of, paid directly or indirectly.** Is this possible now? Expectation for finding jobs today is negligible. The daily news paints a negative scenario for obtaining jobs: quantity or quality not feasible, so use "down time" to prepare for the future jobs you will desire. Look for free training programs, I've listed some for **you.**

UNFORTUNATELY, the few jobs that are available at the higher levels of many businesses and industrial enterprises have VERY high tech, high pressure, high volume responsibilities, not feasible for beginners. It is to understand large scale illustrations, with many other complex multi-stranded job requirements, and knowledge to break them down into logical workable sequences. Using analogies with familiar items and events, and melding them with straight forward language; these jobs require vast amounts of varied experience and will instinctively become more complicated for you to acquire and perform well as a newly recruited employee, mainly because of new technological advances. Be smart, you do **not** want to start here! It is strategically too far out!! "It's survival for the fittest." Motivate and prepare yourselves. Have an internal dialogue with **"you"** and pray about outcomes and your job decisions.

PROTOCOLS-For High Schools and College Graduates' checking into the Job Markets. I will **now list important on-the-job protocols. AVOID Taking Things Personally**. In a people-oriented job, you will encounter human emotions at one time or the other. Don't give the manager or workers ammunition to fuel negative feedback regarding your capabilities, knowledge, people skills or communication skills. Are you prepared **technologically?** This is where the knowledge-based emphasis is indicated to provide **the services** and production that will be required of you in the 21ST CENTURY Business community. "**Technical knowledge is power in the here and now.**"

IMPERATIVES FOR SUCCESS:

YOU are being provided here and now with a very comprehensive listings of the **how, when, where, what, and why's** of normal and expected behavior, etiquette and protocol, inherent in all business cultures. This is a **"know before you go assignment . . . . It is a fact, Knowledge is power."**

.. ATTEND free workshops and seminars at any nearby Community College, Job Service Centers, Job fairs, etc. Many free ones are provided by the **Federal government Retraining Programs for some displaced employees,** and for help with resumes' job applications in Employment Offices.

.. UPDATE your credential and resume. Acquire **new Technical Skills. It's a job passport. Build on whatever expertise you already have.** Above average Technical skills are needed to compete. It is a necessity not an option in today's job markets.

.. SHOW INITIATIVE on your resume. Invest in self growth. Volunteer, understudy, be willing to fill in and substitute. Keep your eyes and ears open to learning. It will be considered at interview and if an offer is extended, you could earn incremental awards for motivation and ambitions.

.. ASK FOR LEARNING OPPORTUNITIES - Most large companies have training programs for high school grads whereby you can understudy an expert in certain areas, and be provided with mentors. Be visible, reach out into large companies in nearby communities.

.. DEVELOP transferrable skills that will give some portability to your career interests. Invest in Information Technologies and sciences; the future **is knowledge and service-based employment; a recurring** concept of reality for job security that will have establish itself, perhaps, permanently.

.. BE RESULTS ORIENTED. Always put your goal in writing so you can streamline your objectives as necessary, and as life experiences teach you wisdom, or how to survive. Economic fluctuation happens every four or five years, so up-grading skills should be a long term objective.

.. Meet the challenge as they come along. "The CREAM" that rises to the top is not characterized by any routine or superficial means. This person is pragmatic, self-motivated and very prepared to succeed in the job markets of science and technology or as a Solo-entrepreneur.

THE CREAM in this Book is not about personality or genealogy. We are not a machine to be fixed or a problem to be solved. Exactly who then, you may be wondering; a progeny, a geek? As described, **The cream** is a self-motivated, innovative, talented and technically astute person who will succeed using all the new viral/technical knowledge and skills, communication logistics gadgets, necessary marketing skills, keen sense of team responsibility, perseverance, and who has the necessary tools to grow and advance.

YOUR inalienable blueprint identifies and differentiates you from everyone else who evolves through creation. The DNA that we got at birth does not make us into a prince or a pauper, nor does your lineage. **We** determine who or what we want to be. These intrinsic prototype or uniqueness minimally defines your destiny and only motivation and the need for survival will help to steer you above the plateau of **ordinary to the extraordinary**. Only then your true identity will be revealed as a **cream, the one who will rise to the top**. Despite the identifying genetic markers you were given at birth, you will have to add the ingredients to rise - that is, **true motivation**. "A cake will not rise without some yeast."

This is all so relevant for today's speed of change. We have to capture and assess the full spectrum of where we are, define how to meet the challenges and invest in finding and seizing opportunities bought about by the change.

THE WORLD is constantly changing and the workplace changes along with it. Work is gone viral and international and the transition is permanent. A little intensity will keep us alert and vigilant to begin a brand new process of figuring out how to establish better control of what is now, and what is to come. There is a an enigma, "It is better to experience life than to analyze it," or we can resolve to simplify some resulting problems by using a math operation strategy to conjure a balanced approach! Within the continuum of the economic downturn, many people may entertain the possibility of another genre of work. Confucius said, "SUCCESS depends upon previous preparation and without such previous preparation, there is bound to be failure." Preparation and motivation is the key.

MANY workers have transition from White Collar to the so-called Blue Collar work to maintain personal and family responsibilities. We did not see the creeping of the depression toward us in 1998 and 1999. **(I will not divert your attention here to the coming of the collapse of American prosperity.**) This is not the theme of this book. My emphasis here is to encourage workers to prepare, grow, succeed, and be the best "CREAM of the crop." **Be prepared is both declarative and imperative in these uncertain times of perpetual change**. This is well documented in my book entitled "SURVIVAL." **A decade ago, a perceptive vision of the crises was promulgated vividly by Mead.**

The Global Economic Crisis - as written by Walter Russell Mead, was written at the beginning of the global economic crisis of 1997-2000, (which unfortunately is the prediction for today's catastrophe), which is indeed not a historic event. I **see the same occurrences today** with worsening impacts on family life, essential securities, Banking, unemployment, loss of homestead, millions of unemployed people, and an overall despair and lack of confidence in the American Federal budgetary, planning and financial systems. This is certainly "an economic cataclysm as big as or bigger than the Great Depression of the 1930s." Who would have guessed that the developed world, Asia and the European Union would suffer deflationary debts and banking crisis that hasn't yet reached its end.

THE long period of American expansion and prosperity is probably over. **But it is not all about us. The real worries, depression and joblessness are now everywhere; it's now global. "IT'S THE ECONOMY STUPID!" (The favorite quote from former President, Bill Clinton).** The effects are devastating in every area of human existence. **WE ARE THERE!** We were certainly not prepared for the losses we are enduring, and preparation to rise above them are slow and frustrating. But **THE CREAM** cannot be held down it must rise to the top. It's natural, it's human, it's inevitable and "HE or SHE" will still be at the top when jobs in America are back in vogue. Very soon, I hope, let's pray and be optimistic! Wall Street stocks are still rolling significantly downwards with negative prediction for the near future. **There is no "feel good" factor for the "Global Risk markets."** Today's news report posits that 17 European countries' employment rate is about 55 percent. This is hard **for graduates** who have nothing to fall back on. No need to ask why many 27 year olds plus, are living with their parents or relatives who can accommodate them.

YOU may have also experience tremendous loss and failure in your life, but be positive and not be overcome by it. "Quitting is not an option and dreams do not have deadlines or expiration dates." You are young, healthy, curious, so push aside limitations and liabilities and continue to evolve and grow. Greet every day as a chance to begin something new, make a wish and make sure that wish comes true. Look forward to significance by updating your business and technical courses to achieve remarkable success sooner or later, whether you work for a corporation or become a Solo Entrepreneur. All work components have gone viral, and you cannot be unprepared to compete and jeopardize your life's goal. **Keep developing and demonstrating your higher level thinking skills**. Here are some of the specific mindset for writing this book.

THE BOOK is developed as a roadmap, a compass, a close companion for job preparation, hunting, finding, progressing and hopefully, for references and check points throughout your working life and beyond. Each section contains my personal encouragement, concepts, principles, techniques ideas, private and government policies and notations gleaned from work experiences. The knowledge you gain and display can be an integral and constructive objectives and skills set goal for your professional development. **Your attitude can either nourish and encourage your personal and professional growth or undermine and sabotage them.** The principles of affirmation, using the **process of feedback and its evaluative applications to every job position has become a clear pragmatic guideline requisite for work establishments.** So as you prepare for this journey of self-growth, it is very important that you orient yourself properly. The poor economic situations have resulted in Negative Feedback frenzies in most workplaces, conspired by job insecurities. Be aware of its corrosive nature and its growing propensity in the market place. **Be advised!**

JOB MARKET RESEARCH

When you are comfortable that you have accomplished putting the pieces of preparation together, as reiterated before, then you can focus on identifying by the process of elimination, the best prospects **for your skills and/or career interests. Know your markets by networking, research and by the following processes:**

- Identify companies at specific locations and their competition, having your job interests.

- Research targeted agencies for size, census, employee retention, and annual reports.

- Revisit your qualifications to see if you are a match for their product and services.

- Conduct on-line market researches on your targets - enlisted businesses or industries.

- Do some networking by developing close insider relationships. Knowing the right people is important when you are dealing with a complex bureaucracy.

- Your contact persons can point you to new opportunities and make sure you are at the right place at the right time.

- Seek out opportunities where you know you can perform well. Do not refuse temporary or substitute assignment. It may become permanent. At large companies, you can suggest volunteering, or make known your desire to understudy in a particular department that matches your career interest. Many full-time positions have been gained by starting in temporary positions.

After you have completed updating your qualifications and research into organizations that could possible use your talents and skills, then you will begin to design a resume' to send (fax) to these places. FAXING first is the new deal. If there is a match or fit for a job, they'll call you for an interview. An application form must accompany the resume. While you are awaiting! Waiting! and waiting! **for that call,** do some practice interviews. You may be able to find something on line if you are a first-time employee. If you are, I will give you a "heads up."

IN THE INTERVIEW, if you are asked about any negative situation that you have incurred in the past, even at school, **and if it's true, own it.** Don't be surprised if you are aptly informed about them. Employers are also researching. Some questions usually asked are:

..What do you know about our company?

..Why did you take six months away from school?

..Describe yourself with one adjective?..

..Where do you see yourself in five years?

..Why do you want to work for us?

IN this age when multiple facets of information can be extracted from the media and technology sources, there are no secret gardens. Feedback, positive or negative, blooms in every niche of society, in fertile business office, and more so, when jobs are scarce, and competition is fierce for jobs and all things connected to it. You must be **decisive** and intentional when you are thinking about interviewing for employment. **Influence** the people you meet, know the art of greeting, handshake, giving app**ropriate complements.** Make a **positive and lasting impression on all the interviewers.** They are the ones who recommend you to managers for the appropriate job that matches your skills set.

OTHER important facts and detail you need are: **Know as much about the Company as you can before you interview**. Dumpster dive, Google, Network, insider proxy. Also know: Name of President, CEO, COO, size of the Company, Pay scales, Employee retention history, traditional or conventional. Is the company private, government, agency, union, international, Institution, etc. Ask if they provide employees handbook, and Benefits Booklet. Impress the interviewers with your knowledge and quest for technical skills set, and the new viral communication applications and gadgets. Show them how to make high-tech gadgetry more user friendly. **Blow them away, without being eccentric! (boastful). Be a cream!** Check on free Employment Training Seminars, near you. A record of excellent performance in your interview, and positive feedback from schools or former jobs, are your passport for a job. Today's job prospects may depend on a compilation of favorable feedback from all or most of the interviewing sources. **Your first impression should be lasting. My suggestion is: Get "A" job and rise up through gradual progression. Knowing how to demonstrate your abilities and higher level thinking skills are crucial.**

GETTING ("A",) ("ANY"), ("THE") JOB. BUSINESSES are responding to the priorities and challenges of the digital age and are co-opting all the dynamic technologies coming down the pipe. You must have knowledge, expertise talent and be prepared, if you want to have job success and stability. Now, you have got a job. **You need to know** the coincidences of changing environment, circumstances and responsibilities; you will be on your own to make decision for completing all duties within prescribed timing limitations.

.. Intelligence is multifaceted and can be expressed in many ways. You must have the compelling need to go beyond minimum competency. **Show your smarts from day # 1.**

.. Internet communication techniques are giving us world-wide connectivity. Invest your energy in finding and seizing all opportunities for which you are qualified here or abroad. Many large American corporations and industries have businesses in other countries.

.. **Your job description has your signature on it. Do whatever it takes, morally, to get the job done**. Your desire to succeed must supersede your fear of failure. The larger test is working with a team leader "Who knows every thing" and also has a positive attitude and agenda to help new employees succeed.

.. **Guard your integrity** and the competency you have achieved so far. These will be your passport to progress. Always scrutinize your work first, before submitting it to your boss.

.. **Your game plan should be SURVIVAL**. The first six months is critical, for review of attitude, talent, people skills, time management, accuracy, team connection. Embrace and give positive feedback regarding company interests.

.. **Work at your commitments** objectively and with a smile, and get job progression the hard way "**earn it.**" You can exchange hard work for smart work, but don't make it look easy! Be kind, offer help when needed, and be courteous and respectful to peers and managers alike.

.. **Meet the challenges;** do not resist change, you will be disqualified, be aware that all organizations need to compete to have a share in the marketplace. Don't be concerned with the unimportant. You need to showcase your expertise and become a valuable and indispensable employee. **Manage your career!**

.. To reiterate, new job markets **require initiative** on your part to fulfill the job requirements that you signed on to. **It is a contract** and you can't simply sit back and wait for your manager to discover your smarts. You must use knowledge, momentum, accuracy and confidence to quietly communicate and distinguish yourself. There is a saying, "**Blossom where you are planted.**"

.. **Try to be adaptable** and willing to change job positions, without question if and when you are interdepartmentally transferred. Embrace the challenge. Usually, change can be a positive opportunity for learning new skills, getting showcased, more money and promotion.

.. This is the stage where **you must show yourself flexible. Success** comes from being passionate about your skills, talents and filling the need wherever the job is, in the company's head office, outsourced to a field office or overseas; go if family is not a negative factor.

.. Change is not comfortable but more often than not, when there is personal development involved, the outcome can be favorable and invariable become your positive exposure to higher tiers.

.. **Find ways to grow**, be part of a team that is positive, and research widely for new options through workshops, community college training programs, networking on line; get "linked-in."

There is no progress limitation for those who are willing to reinvent themselves in order to meet the demands from top echelon. **The** CREAM

enters here. Local growth industries are not limited to hiring four-year degree graduates. To get preference for jobs in those upper level tiers, you must first understand the environments, develop teamwork intervention strategies, have the capabilities, **and a positive feedback press.** Remember if you have **the propensity to be the CREAM, you will rise.**

EMPLOYEES ON/OFF JOB Volunteering. It is a concept that you may consider when applying for a new job or existing position, is your belief and involvement in Volunteering in your neighborhood or even in your work assignment area. If you add that nugget to your profile it will give you a considerable edge to be considered for college entrance and/ or job opportunity. Eleanor Roosevelt said, "The true riches of life, I think, is a sense of having fulfilled some needs of others." (I volunteered all through colleges and work, and I still volunteer today as an advocate for healthcare and other social issues for the needy.)

VOLUNTEERING is a natural spontaneous response to a need for service wherever and whenever, without any financial interest, receipt or value consideration. It is a leading indicator of your sense of responsibility, citizenship and good character. From experience and inductive reasoning, an employer can logically infer that you would manage and be successful in your chosen field. While there is much to gain through hard work and doing more than is expected of you, the reverse is you have much to lose through inertia, apathy or laziness.

BEING a volunteer can reflect positively in favor of your capacity for work and can help to keep the flame of your enthusiasm intact. It's a **"feel good thing!"** And in this new phase of a long economic downturn, you are subject to your environment. Therefore, select a positive environment that will best develop your character, desired objectives and successful lifestyle. The fire of your enthusiasm will be extinguished unless it is refueled, so relate, assimilate and use these principles to motivate others and keep your flame alive. Focus on the success formulas you have acquired from volunteering and incorporate them in your daily activities in route to be the CREAM.

IT IS GOOD, that we **humans** are at the apex of evolution, with the potential to control nature and bend it to serve our purposes. The new requirements for employment prospects may depend on a compilation of favorable feedback from all or most of these sources where you have worked or volunteered. A track record of excellent performance can lead to progressively larger awards on the job. The way that job specifications, performance and evaluation criterion or statements of work appraisal, character and your credit rating get communicated is through various channels of feedback from all or most personnel resources. Also, know that sometimes requisites for feedback fails to reflect reality accurately.

.. **At this** juncture, I assume that you have a working knowledge of all web communications and other VIRAL (virtual) TECHNOLOGIES.

.. **Identify** the product knowledge or services you can offer any company that may hire you.

.. **Know how** to build a support network system that will provide you with positive feedback. Display your proclivities for hard work and regard for protocols of respect for all.

.. **Focus on knowing** how to integrate, balance and complete work within the company's time frame. In businesses, time is of the essence.

.. **Seek out job opportunities** for positions where you know you have some experience, the skills set required, being on time, and perform well within your capabilities. Also:

Hope is not elusive, being the Cream is very attainable. The ultimate reward is achieving a state of enlightening in a new job, new place, new people. You are establishing your new career and it has consequences, positive and negative; it's all in the game plan that requires a unique cultural, perspective, dedication and cooperation. Your entry into the workforce means **you have a signed contract by way of your job description. Keep it close to you for the first few weeks to review as necessary.**

.. **Be intentional to successfully** accomplish all assigned work. It is contribution that counts! The value added is the extra work you do; make a difference. Use those proclivities to excel and progress, thus leaving a trail of good references behind for others to emulate. Model these good habits for those you intend to manage!

.. **Eliminate unnecessary steps** in producing and completing assigned work unless you are given a step-by-step option. If not, use your smarts. Usually the bottom line is what matters. **Therefore focus on the results not on the process**! Review carefully before submitting.

.. **Build strong relationships** with internal and external clients. Anticipate their needs and be responsive to requests that are line items of your job. Do some teambuilding for job knowledge.

.. **Embrace change, it will be a constant**! Fresh ideas, new insights plus practical skills are always a good combination for progress. **Always seek managers advice first, if needed.**

.. **Be responsible for your morale and attitude always.** Be very mindful to promote positive feedback for others and company daily.

.. **Don't focus on the procedural risks** you've taken to fulfill a task. At the end of each business day, affirm yourself as courageous.

.. **Positive affirmations do work** if you commit to them. You can be all you want to be - the **CREAM** indeed. **Believe in teamwork**, it's a necessity not an option and you should work to maintain it. It will be mentioned at your job evaluation time and propagate to supervisors.

.. If your actions inspire others to dream more, learn more and become more, you will make your niche as a desirable and valued employee. Appraise the company positively, even if you are not asked for an assessment or overview.

IT IS EASY to roll your eyes and feel helpless and annoyed when faced with a seemingly insurmountable problem. Challenges are as daily as life is, and must be treated as real life experiences. **Here are some truths that are nuggets for all ages:**

* "You can't change the direction of the wind.
* The world is constantly changing and the workplace changes along with it.

* A little intensity keeps you alert and vigilant.
* **WHY** is like a seed when planted, produces a balanced approach.
* Inspiration and solution are necessary, but it is important to be able to tell the difference.
* Business, as usual, is not sustainable.
* Teamwork is a product of two ingredients, communication and experience.
* Life Bumps - personal or economical - not infrequently upend our world. But the optimist - the CREAM increasingly finds rewarding second acts.
* The past doesn't predict the future.
* Values are tested in times of financial stress.
* Individuals must make several practical decisions and continue aggressive efforts to rise to greatness."

AS A WHOLE new genre of depressed **generation, you must find a purpose to rise above adversity**. Despite all the changes taking place around us, our mandate must remain the same; that is, find a purpose, and the right way to do the right thing. **Take everyone who is prepared for excellency with you and influence a whole new genre of workers who want to succeed and rise up. It is hard to generalize, but let's just stipulate that less than 50 percent of workers have embraced self-interest to go back or forward to be ahead of the future, or take time to** reclaim their idealism or goal and redirect in a way that can bring greater contributions and meaning to their lives. **YOU ARE THERE, Congrats! You have risen! You are a cream!**

NOW, what is the barrier to the job and financial success that you deserve? Is it time, lack of preparation, or is it the economy? You have to take action and stop being a procrastinator or spectator. Reading this book, totally, will give you the answers to overcome challenges, eliminate roadblocks and accelerate your ambition and profession. I'll **transition now to the second imperative that is, to speak to all unemployed workers.**

FEEDS FOR UNEMPLOYED WORKERS, PROFESSIONALS, SPECIALISTS, et al.

"NOTHING IN THE WORLD CAN TAKE THE PLACE OF PERSISTENCE. TALENT W ILL NOT; NOTHING IS MORE COMMON THAN UNSUCCESSFUL PEOPLE WITH TALENT. EDUCATION WILL NOT; THE WORLD IS FULL OF EDUCATED DERELICTS. PERSISTENCE AND DETERMINATION ALONE ARE OMNIPOTENT. THE SLOGAN "PRESS ON" HAS SOLVED AND ALWAYS WILL SOLVE PROBLEMS OF THE HUMAN RACE."

- Calvin Coolidge.

THIS is such an applicable and logical premise/ anecdote for such a time as this, so evident in today's workplace and everywhere people exist. That is, **Determination** alone will crush this pervasive anomaly known as the economic downtrend or crisis, and its concurrent depression causing unprecedented emotional stress in every arena of life for Americans. There is a global disbursement of economic infeasibility so the problem is every where. It is fundamentally a basic analyses of cause and effect in all instances of surviving conditions of unemployment and homelessness.

THE DEFICIT problems are evident in work places and causes deprivation in every human existence. Economic **changes will require planned determination, responsible management and combined high-level collaboration with international innovative "think-tanks" to help crush this pervasive anomaly.** Among the bitter ironies of the down-trending of our economy, many countries are in similar situations, and our com**panies are advertising and extending job offers to people**

who are currently working and not to the unemployed! Their two methods of approach is the inclination to ignore what is, in contemplation of what should be. The fundamental divergence remains between those who see this action as a lack of ethics and those who regard it as a vehicle of power. This is discouraging to the unemployed; but be proactive, be aggressive, contrive a different approach to get the attention of employers. You have to know how to dance to their music.

I agree the workforce has shrunken in many companies, but this is not a new phenomenon. It happened in the 1980s, 1990s and 2000s but is incomparable to the current reported statistics. My background in Business and Education has infused in me the passion to provide you with some helpful insights, actionable and positive suggestion for success, because there is a difference between appearance and reality, which can reveal both positive and negative dimension in the world of work.

While you are waiting on a job offer, engage yourself in doing something as a solo-entrepreneur or a social service **volunteer helping the needy or take** some free essential technical courses at a Community college continuing education class. You must be proactive and intentional to combat the negativities of being out-of-work for two years or more. Being engaged implies that you are very interested in working, that you realize that hard/smart work is the most desirable road to success, **"that yesterday was what it was, today is what it is, and tomorrow is what it will be,"** and that you approach **every** work with care, passion and motivation, talent and proven technical abilities.

BEING motivated implies that you are very interested in what you are doing; recognize its importance to any company, and your ambition and drive to fulfill your goal; (**don't ever let go of your life's goal despite the present circumstances**). Always be decisive and flexible **to go with the flow** on any job you are given. Avoid negative feedback, and its pervasive ramifications, and try to gain the advantage of receiving the promotions that you will have earned. Know that a company can create a moral environment which portrays a distinct set of values and standards to which it holds its employees accountable. Managers operate with a realistic view of a future with acquired profit propensity for their company, a condition that is better in some important ways than what currently exists. Every employee's task is to enable that propensity. These are essential nuggets gleaned from my experience.

The Guidelines listed herein for Surviving the economic downturn have been developed to help you discover important concepts and to encourage you to develop the capabilities to meet the new marketing and working skills for the Twenty-First Century, and this decade in particular. Numerous examples of the pros and cons are supplied, and readers are urged to select and record applications from these inferences that will fit their own particular personality, style, situations and needs. These inferences promote honesty for experiencing the issues so pervasive in the workplace today. **A chance to shine spotlight on the negative aspects of unemployment is very noteworthy.** As I am writing today, there are several groups of activists in many large cities in America that are amassing sit-downs, so-called "Flash Mobs" protesting the joblessness and its subsequent effects on life in general. The poor and affected are relegating the current situation to the "greed of the rich and privileged" as compared to the poor and needy, **and the need for prioritizing policies to keep the United States mostly at middle-class status.**

As the veil of stability and optimism falls under economic adversity, we all need to have a survival mentality and have an exceptional impact on the motivation of those who will be **the cream that rises** and, will hopefully, work toward the demise of social injustice in employment and compensation. Not committing to a more daunting hopefulness but believing that you can help, if given a job that will create greater prosperity, consolidate management and employee-relations, while on the other hand, realizing that CHANGE can cause discomfort, and can be tentatively paralyzing. But when RULES are in place to be executed as a process, you must apply yourself accordingly. As a matter of fact, only by working with the principles and techniques for surviving over a period of time that your extraordinary efficacy can be clearly seen and appreciated. If you are a CREAM, impress peers and employees with the logic of your position to help, and the confidence with which you respect the company's rules for personnel relations. You will begin to live in harmony with the universe and make your years of working experience a plus rather than a minus in your diary or autobiography.

IF YOU are an Experienced, Professional or Specialist employee, who unfortunately have been under/or unemployed for whatever reason, you are aware of the profound difficulties this economic downturn has impacted your motivation, your lifestyle and ambition. If you are 55 years+ your jobless rate has more than doubled since the recession began four years ago. Misconceptions about older workers abound. I have read of a 57year old who after 36 years lost her Bank job to downsizing, and after a year and 257 applications which yielded 2 interviews and no job offers. There are many stories of bad experiences today. Sometime ago, downturn merely punctuated a strong rising trend such as the market friendly years of 1983-2000. People invested in homes and diversified investments and were not really conservative with money, and are now being squeezed from all ends. Who would have guessed that the developed world would suffer such deflationary debts, in banking, housing, business and industry. It's a defining crisis and **"WE ARE THERE"** - but with hope that The YEAR 2012 will defy the inevitable and bring a semblance of renewed prosperity to all depressed and desolate peoples of the U.S and the world.

TO transition from an initial surviving phase to the current phase, and effects of an economy that is responding to hiring people of your caliber and expertise will be negligible. There is, and will be a new trend to enhance profitability and decrease projected operating expenses. Because of lessons learned in the current situations, this may not be positive or encouraging dialogue, **but you must be willing to upgrade every skills you have and try to acquire new ones to have an above-average competitive edge in these uncertain times.**

Analyze and compare all your core competences against specific markets, and develop a clear understanding of the ways their goods and services positively benefit their clients. Take a proactive approach and develop a plan to meet and beat their prospective system upgrade. Take your plan, resume' and an application to the Operating Manager, let him/her know you have done your research and you are aware of progressive upgrades that are commensurate to the company. Ask for a follow-up meeting to discuss your application for the job **and bring your "show and tell."** Develop a plan that is unique to that company, (as you have researched). Use the dialogue in the concept of a Webinar so it can be shown and discussed with CEO's and upper management teams. Project yourself with an attitude of competency and knowledge. "Human affairs in business and industry can be directed and modified when human thoughts and action are not void of purpose." You may appropriate your new job in a very short time!

THESE IMPERATIVES are for new hires!

WE work, no matter the force of conventional eventualities. In most cases, working can be a joyous encouraging thing, a security blanket. It means there may be full employment for those who stay aware of the goals of their employers, and are sensitive to making that organization successful. Lasting success however, is not the result of coincidence but the result of smart and focused hard work. **Consider being the cream that rises. But success is never a one-man's job, it takes team work.** So count your blessings that you are, or will be a part of that inspirational group of workers who are inwardly motivated and simply enjoy playing the game, and always want to play to win in what they can do, when the economy fully recovers. Always **create positive energy on the job**. Lack of it creates an implication for discovery of failure in performance because it fails to provide grounds for purposive and meaningful action.

ENERGY ebbs and flows in life and in all activities. The elements of distraction are often influenced by events which have no essential connection with your job at all. Do not regard a lull in tempo to be consistent. This is the time **to draw new energy and focus on your job at hand**, to get managers attention that you are EXTRAORDINARY and that you are not constrained by winter blues, summer heat or any negative feedback! The belief that certain facts are unalterable, and that certain trends are lifelong are not a true statement. Be a CREAM. Every age claims the right to create its own values and passes judgment in light of them.

NOW that you are employed, (in whatever capacity) take advantage of the company's programs and initiatives to train and support its employees. Some offers a variety of flexible work-on-the-job-training arrangements that are used to accommodate diverse personal situations such as returning to school for an advanced degree, or technical enhancements programs. In an on-going effort to establish and maintain a workplace that values and leverages its employees to their maximum potential, large companies are looking at innovative recruitment and hiring practices, and the adequacy of their information network and adding new technical gadgets. Some of these companies' employee publications feature management commitment and accountability to their employees.

AS BEST PRACTICE, large employers emphasizes the importance of comprehensive multifaceted planning to attract and retain world-class employees. The uniqueness and innovativeness of their programs implemented for recruitment and hiring policies, programs, and practices are evidence of their effort to retain the best qualified and motivated applicants. **They have planned workforce accommodation for those employees with disabilities and special needs. Feedback is encouraged by managers to update employees progress at regular intervals to assess if** training needs are necessary and are **provided.**

COMPANIES may also have career management booklets focusing on careers in each department that explain what is needed in terms of performance, technical skills and education for each step of job progression. If you work in a cultural diverse organization they may introduce inter-relationship practices in order to encourage workforce diversity. This is a company that is sensitive to the needs of all employees, and aim at providing skills and job opportunity, will have a one-to-one meeting with all new employees to discuss entry level positions and scholarships, and perhaps, that after one-year training on the job, they can apply for a transfer. To understand fully that the corrosive effect of harassment on morale (negative feedback and gossip are included), non-productivity, all employees engaged in these activities are subjected to disciplinary measures including dismissal. **All these notations are a heads-up for you to ask questions in a job interview.** This book is being advisedly written for your job interviews, retention and success. Make notation of all practical information.

FOR YOUR **Personal and Career Development, take advantage of semina**rs, work-shops, training seminars offered or sponsored by your company, or even diverse ones offered by the competition (be discreet). You may be able to bring something new or different to the table at your company. Do not neglect opportunities to learn and grow. Free Training workshops offered by Community Colleges in your area, and the Federal Government Workforce offices in most counties also provide retraining and job preparation help for displaced, laid-off, non-employed workers for free or low cost. **Most private Universities get funding for community based business owners and those are also free**. Remember education is a constant life process. Modern technocratic industries do not accept excuses; it's imperatively indicated in all job requisites that new hires be technically prepared for the jobs. Whatever the goal or profession you chose in life cultivate the following mantra: "If you want it, you can achieve it; if you can dream it, you can become it." Keep in mind, Confucius's perspective on **PREPARATION** for success.

OUTLINE what you and the employer agreed upon in your job description at the time of hire. In your first evaluation feedback sessions, at 3 months, 6 months or 1 year, whatever the interim. Tell him/her what you have contributed to the company so far, and what you envision can be accomplished successfully in the future. Express what you see as viable steps that the company are taking to increase profitability and things that are impacting employees positively. You have moved around and are convinced you would like to continue to work for the company for a long time. In this dialogue, you may be asked to discuss your feelings about the operations of the company. Please **Appraise the company in a positive way**, even if you are not asked for an overview! Be truthful, do not mention anything negative - that is a not-so-good strategy. Hold onto those feelings until you become a manager!! If that is your CREAMY ambition, GO FOR IT!!

NO matter what situation may arise, know that good times are often offset by bad times, it is a fact of life. Before you react negatively, use good judgment. Smile even when you are feeling miserable, overwhelmed, unappreciated. Take control of every possible job situation, (some are designed to test your coping skills). Put them in vogue as learning experiences and move on to what is ahead. When you take positive action, you accomplish great tasks, work, goals, dreams, interpersonal skills, career fulfillment and are mentally prepared for any-thing that could be a surprise for someone else. Today, more than ever before, when a business invests capital to hire, it may ask a prospective employee: **"What is the payback for this investment?"** How you answer this question can be the catalyst for the job offer. Do some research into the workings of the company and/or ask a business consultant who is current in his/ her game to develop a concise and well-thought-out response for such a question.

ALL companies are interconnected either by their service providers, their business partners, competitors, or the goods and services they provide. So to be on the upper tier, they have to maintain their passion on a higher playing field. The new solidarity for action steps in the improvement and procurement of state of the art technical machinery, and application of sciences to production that coincide with progress on a global scale, make all turning back impossible. Despite companies' latest innovations, they are not hiring to any recognizable degree. However, people are finding creative ways to support themselves as the internet has leveled the field for access to information about companies, their products and services. Many companies are outsourcing technical support work to people who are qualified and work at home. What you've learned from the internet will help you build a platform from which you can develop a qualifying proposition that will help you differentiate yourself in finding a niche by way of providing a product or service to some established business franchise, or intuitively become a Solo-Entrepreneur.

CAN YOU eliminate the unemployment distractions and consider becoming an Entrepreneur? You may need "Start-up" **money** for a private or partnership business, or you could consider becoming small-business company with funding from the (SBA) Government Small Business Administration. If you chart your course to include government contract, read brochures or check the Web at WWW.MYGCAT.COM, or visit Community colleges in your area to see if they have joined the National Association for Community College Entrepreneurship. Ask for a Brochure. "Positive approaches to the future do offer a glimmer of hope for at least some jobless people. "Solo-E's" are beginning to flourish as people are seizing the opportunity to explore and experience being their own boss. The business climate is still good for the high-tech industry. Solo-E's are professionals who chose to go into business by themselves, collaborate with others, grow their business without boundaries, and more likely without employees." Check on the Web for links to, or in libraries for the following Books: TRADING PLACES, INC., FREE

30

AGENT NATION., THE FUTURE OF WORKING FOR YOURSELF., SOLOENTREPRENEUR.COM, INC., - Daniel Pink." These books are available and they provide a wealth of information.

IF you are interested and capable to use your creativity, talent, background knowledge and patience, the above information is appropriate. **Remember that some changes are good, but all have their challenges.** You have had a **wide** panoply of principles, starting from Page 1 of this book are descriptive recipes, and formulas encapsulated for a practical personal reference strategically arranged as a page-by-page guide. Each page contains usable seasoned knowledge-experienced base contents that will prompt you to take a positive look at how to navigate from here to there, safely and positively. These fundamental principles are proven entities and characterization, to assist you in becoming The CREAM. I have used personal experiences and researched "Best Practices" from Companies reflecting current employment mandates with Job Analysts and Trainers to be up to date on what employers' are doing. I was there once as a trainer. I have done recent research to guide you through the unemployment pilgrimage.

THE ability to interpret the meaning of what you observe, the thoughts that neutralize an undesirable emotion, the indignity of fruitless job searches, the undeterminable length of the current downturn of the economic indicators, and the futility that accompanies its existence in the lives of working Americans, are all being detailed within the pages of this guidebook. Understanding that changes in any arena can cause discomfort is an understatement as you move through a difficult phase of repositioning life. **Fact is, only by working with these advice, principles, techniques and using the tools and guidelines over a period of time that the poignant strategies for solving the problems to rise up and become the CREAM can be clearly seen and appreciated.**

SO much of what we do is conveyed by example. My privilege has been to observe both from afar and close what dedication, integrity and faith looks like; how they are lived out very day. In a culture that has become self-centered, it is refreshing and intriguing to witness **a real-life model that will reach up and not leave others behind**. Always remember those whose shoulders you may be standing on to "reach up." In this large and diverse population, **a blanket suggestion for everyone to rise above the ground level to the upper echelon is a misnomer,** when there are people with many forms of disabilities, specific, intellectual, or physical. **My desire is to discuss the importance of providing encouragement to those who have the capacity to learn, create, progress and succeed to help others.** Some people may have weaknesses in the mind or body and their behaviors are sometimes seen as being weird, abnormal or bizarre. They are not to be exploited, seen as non-humans or be disregarded because of those special or basic needs. **Be kind to all along the upward journey so that you will see your signature on them later in a better situation, if and when Providence, luck or medicine erased the past.**

PEOPLE in our culture have been taught that life is all about getting ahead and getting things for themselves. Motivate those who are merely involved to move above the standard of normal, to model extraordinary or excellent ways. If motivation is a stimulant we are preparing you to transcend and make a living - **a vibrant display of what a cream is all about. You have surmount the mundane and rise to being one cream of the human race. This precious truth can change lives forever.** In the course of many conversations, it has become clear to me that this way of understanding is precisely a part of being who you want to be. How can we grow in our ability to succeed when we are being so self-focused? A natural human tendency is to reach up and leave others behind. This is a dilemma and I am hard pressed to imagine any other solution than for you to be rational, not a "disconnect" in a diverse community of workers. Support and appreciation can be life changing for all of us.

THIS generation has constant conversation but minimal connections. Today, they are on line on social medias, texting, tweeting - **they really aren't forming deep relationships at home, school or at work. They need mentors**. In order for young people to become autonomous adults, they must learn resiliency from their own troubling situations wherever they exist. Disengagement from social contacts on the job makes them vulnerable to defection because they never developed coping practical ways of citizenship. This protracted time of "rootless" living hardly encourages consistent involvement in social environments. Although young adults today are some of the most creative, innovative, and passionate to ever have walk on the planet. The challenge is to provide opportunities for development in community-based activities to this new non-relational generation because they are so vulnerable to deflection as they never developed any sense of stability. They see a disconnect between the current economic situation, as a divergence from what the government says, and what it does. This feeling of despondent malaise is transferred into the workplace and perhaps some positive conversations of support and appreciation may be life changing for them. It may take years of strong impact for any one of them to rise as a cream.

YOU know you are a Cream when you have a good paying, up-scale job in a bad economy. **YOU ARE THERE!** To stay on top, however, means you have prominence and must accrue staying power from those who got you there. A little intensity will keep you alert and vigilant only for a short time. So, begin a brand new process of figuring out how to establish better control when employers squeeze every minute of work from you daily. **You are a CREAM and you are there!** Take five-minute breaks when necessary to engage your mind with off-the-job scenarios:

.. **"Inject a** sense of urgency into current events by using creative thoughts in the middle of a situation. **Imagination creates energy.** That energy will translate to a finished project.

.. **Bring** in intriguing news articles that leave you with unanswered questions, it will keep your connected to outside happenings.

.. **Use reasoning.** See yourself discovering . . . something new that could bring insight and spotlight to clarify a problem project.

.. **Encourage** and engage yourself in adding missing facts and inventing solid outcomes. - Resolve to simplify the problem. Use a math operation strategy. As for logistics, you may have already done the math. **"Why?"** Why is like a seed, when planted produces a balanced approach to sowing and reaping.

SETTING A NEW AGENDA - You are there! Let your work define who you are.

IN the current setting, do a self-assessment. Ask yourself the following questions:

.. Am I empowered by experience, talent or knowledge or desire only to be the best?

.. Am I on the path to growth, achievements, job interests, and do these match my projected objectives and life's goals, or do I need to redefine my ambition for such a time as this?

.. Do I have a connection on the job to what I have learned, and am I measuring up to other workers, or am I seen only as the CREAM?

.. Do I fit in well with others in the community of workers by sharing learned strategies?

.. Does my personal diary contains satisfactory accumulations of any dynamic and ongoing job assessment reflective of sustained progress?

.. Does any application of my job description show progress, effort, achievement, growth, or the ability to apply knowledge or entertain another genre of work in line for management?

AS a result of these considerations, have you developed a fuller understanding of your capabilities, greater appreciation of your work, self, or stronger commitment to learning more dynamics of the job including work in progress, or have you given good ideas and suggestions?

.. Describe how, and what you have done for Company's operation, growth and stability. Will it with stand the scrutiny of an empirical test and will that test appraise your capabilities?

.. Do you agree that cohesive teamwork is the product of communication and experiences?

.. Did you pray about the decisions on your efforts to rise - was it an internal dialogue only?

KNOW you can't change the direction of the wind. The global shifting of the growing economic downsizing and mayhem, in today's workplace operations, will require strong focus, patience, ingenuity and a different approach to move the down trending in an upward direction. When monetary problems become international in scope, and the global economy is so fragile and fragmented, it is futile to opt for genuine collaboration and monetary help from any government in this broad-based recession. For the next economic storm, t**he mantra is** P**reparation! Preparation! Preparation! They come every five years.**

IN my book "SUVIVING THE FEEDBACK FRENZIES," I suggested that all employees, working, laid-off or otherwise get deeply vested with knowledge and virtual skills for the new technological and telecommunication devices that are coming down the pipeline. They sprout **new ones, "you know what" every two years. Learning to use these gadgets quickly, whether or not you like it, you should get on board.** Only the talented, the very shrewd, the fittest, the geek, the **cream** will find good job opportunities on the middle tier when the job market, hopefully, becomes accessible again. Companies that have outsourced abroad are not showing any effort to bring back their jobs to America. It's in their interest and feasibility studies to make profits and **hold them forever!**

IN TIMES like these, my objective is to encourage all the jobless people to, figuratively, fight the challenges with gloves of steel. Wage a war on unemployment - give yourself a year to debrief, regroup, reprioritize, retrain; activate those creative juices, and always accentuate the positive. **Heading back to school?** If Campus life is not for you consider your options and alternatives. **If you are lucky to be working**, model wise use of company time by managing your schedules and commitments. **The future is not a gift, it is an attainment**. Sparking creativity, imagination and innovation is what generated our primary free enterprise system. **Comparison is superficial, do what is right for the company and you will be rewarded. The** best use of time is that which provides stimulation and education, but you also have a primary commitment to engage the culture, grow, and maintaining relationships with others, indulge and encourage them in their personal growth and development to be the CREAM. Then you'll all look to the future with confidence and feel that it was all good!

TRANSITIONING: Experienced employees know that internal consistency within a clearly traditional organization can appear to be in good order as long as most employees can attain the goals they want. Therefore, traditional customs are often highly stable until they wake up to CHANGE. Once they begin to introduce modern technology, their proven methods are threatened and fear of job loss, status, benefits and other insecurities penetrate into the negative feedback loop. Employees will begin to question the new order of operation and expected frustration sets in. The retraining requirements, inconsistencies, the descending order of their employment objectives are factors for discontent. This is the time for you to arm yourself with the facts of YOUR POSITION and all the details relative to the company's new revitalization programs. It means knowing what should be done, what might be done proactively to improve the efficiency of the positions, and of course, the overall stability of the organization in times of constant changes.

AFTER downturn of a once-rising economy, when people feel exploited by all the systems that had contributed to upgrading their life-styles, discontent rises, partly out of fear and lack of communication from upper levels of management. In this situation, allow experience, training and intuition be your guide. This approach can be especially helpful. It is most crucial now, as the **CREAM**, to separate yourself from the disconcerted; react with wisdom and avoid pointless arguments with coworkers. Let your approach, mannerism and positive attitude be your guide. Make a plan with determination **to be in visible control of the situation in words and actions.** Be sensitive, however, to how workers' bad feelings and sensitivity are being compounded and fuelled by the overall recession. The thought of losing employment and moving away from family, friends and perhaps losing a home has a negative impact on them. Be empathetic, but be discreet. Do not engage, encourage, or become distracted by the noise. These are some of the "coincidences that change circumstances."

TAKE CONTROL: Think of your job even with the changes; model an aura of control and positivity in the rising mountains of negativity. It is crucial to separate business from the gossip culture when it's all around you and in every working area. If you see your job as being in a developmental process, you should expect to see yourself ending up somewhere different from where you started. This can be an upward promotion or lateral move. It's all good.

If it's a demotion, it can also be good or bad. You decide . . . "did you work or learn to earn." **Keep your goal in mind**. Take control. Think, feel, perceive and do good. **You are a Cream**. Show initiative, talent, and positive energy daily. In some situations a person grows more often by letting some things go, than by taking some things in. **Don't forget the rights of others; it is how people respond to challenges that matters. Look for the motive behind criticisms. It is said that 99% (percent) of criticism in the form of constructive feed-back from Managers is motivated by a desire to help employees, no matter how caustic and insensitive the criticism may be. Accept the old perpetual adage . . ."No pain, no gain."**

AN employee can benefit from such criticism by accepting it gracefully and try to avoid re-occurrences of it for the same reason or problem. **Develop the capacity for hard, smart accurate work; do more than the work assigned to you each day and make offers to help when there is a need. (This may give you deserved recognition)**. Also make positive decisions about asking for more responsibilities. These are well known career boosting techniques that will condition you to develop "Action Thinking" and capitalize on your business capabilities. Keep a written reserve of up-to-date accomplishment for reference at Evaluation meetings. Without denouncing anyone, make yourself the forerunner for a promotion based on extraordinary performances expected of **a risen CREAM**! Opinions are everywhere and most of them try to pass as facts. To be on the safe side, treat everything you hear as assumptions except proven facts that can be validated. In most organizations, the channels of power and authority shift constantly on the hierarchy. These changes are generally not known until they are announced in a higher level business meeting. The details are then passed on by heads of department to managers and supervisors before workers are informed. Learn vicariously how the organization **works, who decides the details that affect your position.** "Try to understand existing reality and the ways their own standards are rooted in it."

FOR THE SPECIALISTS: You are highly vulnerable in times of economic crises. Unemployment haunt the ranks of hundreds of valued Engineers, Pilots, Machinists and others, laid off from the Space-coast in Central Florida because of truncating of the International Space Program. There are other occupational and health specialists who have also received "pink slips." It is much more difficult to reenter the working environment without feeling that your qualifications and salary outside of your field as fait accompli. Any other field that you may enter is not a comparable fit. **These are other coincidences that change circumstances**: The Federal Government has provided categories of RETRAINING Programs located in most State Unemployment Offices. This is not a feel-good thing for me to relay, but if you have to work it's good to muster some positive energy to reflect that desire, and to distract yourself from negative compromising thoughts. Take the job. **KEEP** on the lookout for new and transitioning programs or business entities moving into your area that may have jobs in your field or otherwise some future wealth creating, math intensive opportunities or in technology fields.

.. Focus on companies with advanced security needs, such as clusters of diverse technical communication updates, digital, viral, emerging technologies that may need some infrastructure workforce and manpower resources to become competitive in the new marketplaces.

.. Look at developing communities that are better equipped, better informed and more committed to stabilizing the depressed economy than any other, which makes you all the more attractive to those who would expand locally or relocate in from other places.

.. High tech, high flex, financially viable, high risk growth companies taking advantage of a wide or complex range of business resources, will be the first to start hiring.

.. Behind every vision, there is an inspiration. This is the stage where you must know yourself. **Reality,** not negativity or doubt must be seen.

.. Remember that fear and doubt is what keep talented people from realizing their life's goals.

.. Enlightenment in skills set concept conjures spontaneous work activities. An employee work ethics is always in unison with the magnitude of his/her production and collaborative work.

.. Interestingly, a new experienced specialist will encounter negative feedback more than anyone else. The more responsibility and greater authority you are given, the more attacks you'll fend off from peers and other workers. Try to show kindness by ignoring these onsets.

ENCOURAGEMENT: Desire to work when work becomes illusive and scarce incurs a cold debilitating feeling. Today, as I am writing, the news is that the job situation in America is not improving. (**There are protests all over the United States to bring attention to the situation**). A few employers are advertising for people who are currently working! What does this mean? Subtle discrimination against all unemployed people whose feelings of disparity and disequilibrium are already morally frayed. Standards like morale and human dignity further disintegrate when businesses deviate from mainstream operating principles.

IT IS not a coincidence when management seem to bend toward budget constraints within their Cost-effective Budgetary Feasibility Plans by not employing experienced or retrained laid-off employees This representation of corporate responsibility of management, (as I knew it,) is seen as inconsiderate lapses in humanity and in their inability to contribute to the wellbeing of the community wherein their company resides. As an employee, your sensitivity to what is unethical and playing out in the marketplace, seems an insult to your integrity, and their irresponsibility to contribute to family and society. It is said, **"all people are victims of society**." Employees, active or inactive, begin to understand in your mind's eye, that **one man's atrophy is another man's progress - be the progressive one!** Job insecurities are not only proliferating excessively in the world, but increasingly so. Can you succeed on your own merit? YES YOU CAN. **Encourage, gravitate upwards, and surprise yourself. It works!**

WHEN you are hired, and if you are a team player, be alive to opportunities, and open to accept and manage critical responsibilities, to accomplish exceptional tasks, to rise above obstacles unscathed and be effective in your expressions in the workforce. Positive feedback from past job may be your passport for a new job. It follows therefore, as a CREAM that you should not align yourself with power gridlock, as you can be of more service with your positive energy without doing so. I think there is just a possibility that at a moment of crisis your talent, peaceful and friendly efforts might make a difference and avert a crisis regarding internal problems. As you read this book, get more wisdom and foresight in the workings of **Corporations**

- known as the real world - you will encounter references specific to your situation. The book has operational guidelines for both employers, new and experienced employees. Be upbeat, encouraged and display positive energy despite your daily anathema. It's life with a new perspective albeit a new decade! (Life can be terrific or horrific!)

NETWORKING and Interviews for ExperiencedCREAMS - Professionals and Specialists: You are the cream who have already risen and want the status and job that you have previously acquired and rightfully so. But times, circumstances and job positions have been compromised by the down-trending economy. You have to be interviewed again and again, and may need some help to compete.

Usually preparation comes before interviews and hiring, and this is a reverse of the normal trend, because for experienced workers, this may be your second "merry-go-round" for new employment consideration in this economy:

.. Conduct on-line searches on companies far or near that best correspond to your job knowledge, interest and expertise. Get some information on their products and services and whether there is international connections. Use network searches, get a copy of their magazine.

.. Your network contacts can point you to new job opportunities and make sure you know the right people, at the right place at the right time.

.. Consider what value you bring to the table that may create a greater perception of you than another candidate. Be ready to showcase your knowledge and /or expertise regarding the new technological components and gadgets. Knowing how to fix broken equipment can add prospective bonus points to your expertise.

.. The technical knowledge you acquire will help build a platform from which relevant questions and conversations can emerge and skills revealed for positive job consideration.

.. Check to see that your credit scores are in good shape and your Face-book portrays positive enlightenments. These are the latest crumple that is creating negative feedback in the job market today for new hires. (Caution).

.. The internet is leveling the playing field as far as access to salary information for certain jobs. **Knowledge is not power until you use it.**

MANY people will tell you to do what you are passionate about. Are all your resources aligned to maximize your strengths? "Success comes from being passionate about FILLING THE NEED; you don't have to be passionate about the need itself." Lisa Rice. Following are other places you may look for jobs: - **Listings on line** - also called **job boards**, - **In newspapers**, local and out of state - "**Jobs not Adds**" Direct Employers Job Search Engines; **BING search engine**; Job centers; Find local listings and apply on line; - **Globaljobsnet.com/employer** - **Employersexpresspros.com**

IN this economic climate, that kind of passion for any job is a panacea - a temporary fix - and should not factor in your life's goal. This distraction will grow dim when your eyes are on the target. You are the CREAM that will rise. Stay true to your desire. Managers with discernment will recognize a valuable employee who can stand on his/her character. A college professor once said "**To be wise is to know reality and then accommodate yourself to it.**"

.. BEFORE THE JOB INTERVIEW: Develop personal relationships and knowing the right people in that enterprise are very important.

.. It takes practical experience which comes from close contact with reality when dealing with a large complex and diverse bureaucracy.

.. Consider interviewing the **"Few"** businesses that are considered to be capital intensive and are not vulnerable to the economic downslide. Get their brochure (overview their census, size, Annual business report and retention history).

.. Getting the job also depend on those favorable feedback you received from a past employer if you have been in the job market before, be sure to mention that fact in the interview.

.. Be responsive to all questions. If they are not clear ask for clarification. Use your experience and research to be courteous and engaging. If questions arise about any bad experience you have had in the past, **and if they are true, answer quickly and affirmatively**. Remember they have your resume' before the interview, and their feedback systems have been deployed prior to the appointment!!

All Job interviewers today are alert for deceptions (Redacted from Personnel Training workshop). Consider these common requests:

- **Tell me about yourself** (talk about education and work experience. Make impressions that you are the best applicant for the job.)

- **Why are you now job searching** (Be honest; I am laid-off. Fired, or a victim of downsizing, economic down-turn, company move, or other)

- Wh**at can you do for us?** (Be prepared. Your research, experience and knowledge of the company's product and services will help to develop the necessary strategies to boost the company's services, goods, profits stability).

- **Tell me about one of your failures**. (This calls for quick thinking. e.g., Using my strength and need for accuracy, I have refused some incomplete and inaccurate assignments from a worker I supervised.)Lastly, but very important:

- **Be proactive in the interview.** Politely and respectfully, ask as much relevant questions as time allows. Make a listing of anticipated questions ahead for such occasions. **This is where competition starts for the job**. You are a Cream, rise to the occasion! **GET THE JOB!**

THE future's not a gift but an attainment. The relationship between appearances and reality of a company's finances, and the past and present economies of scale, make hiring tedious and weigh heavily on employees who are expected to acquire upscale wages. To get a professional job in this economic climate, you may have to sacrifice something from your normal pay schedule. **Take the job**, prove your skills and abilities and pray for a miracle of change for the coming year. Make sure you mention, discreetly, and that the manager perceives you are doing an extraordinary job for the company and are a good example for other employees to emulate.

THE following are EXTRA "things to do and places to go" while you are job hunting. - Convince employers your skills are updated. Stay current with development in your field by reading journals in Business and Industries, etc. - Does your profession have an Association? Are you a member? These groups tend to provide seminars and networking events. Some even offer price breaks to unemployed members. AARP 10/20/10, Carol Fleck. - Check into the updated venerable handbook-**What Color is your** Parachute-Richard Boles - From entry level to seasoned professional, you should be linked to the local and free job search groups, **U.S Labor Department Career - One Stop Organization**, Sate Career development Offices, United Way, Faith based groups, Job Clubs, large churches, synagogues, Chamber of commerce in every state or community. There are stories that an engineer and other professionals have found jobs through interfaith network.

- Look for no-cost job training, or job search assistance, or Career Counseling to help you stay marketable. For experienced workers, Goodwill Centers and AARP offers free advice and training resources including career fairs, resume' and access to employers who value experienced workers **50 years and older.** Check the Web (AARP.org/work) and Goodwill/work.

Employees: Distract yourself from negative counter-intuitive thoughts and reinvent your skills. Maintain a positive attitude. Remember people always bounce back after disasters and personal setbacks with a new outlook and greater appreciation for the things they have had. Reengineer for the next bout of unemployment. Like plagues they come every decade! Know that intelligence is multifaceted and can be expressed in many ways when you have the compelling need to go beyond seeking minimum competency jobs.

"Thousands of people are starting home-based businesses today. These are people of higher value doing self-created work instead of jobs thought up by others. These people work independently and are committed to service, highly flexible, constantly learning and getting better every year." Read - Al Seibert, PhD.

Starting Your Own Business? . . . . There are three things you need to know: 1. Choose a NAME and register the DOMAIN you have associated with the name. 2. Create your Business Entity. You must register your Business Entity and the State. 3. GET AN ATTORNEY. No matter how small the business - Zies, P. Widerman, Malek: StartingYourOwnBusiness@Philip@Legal TeamUSA.Com (by permission).

* If you continue to search for executive level jobs where you can work from home, the business climate for the high tech industry will continue to develop positively because agencies of every type are looking for cost-effective solutions and innovative products to make their business life easier. You are a **Cream, go for it!**

* Check in the monthly **ECONOMIST** under Executive Focus for a few jobs with 6 figure salaries. It's an economic consultancy that assists governments, regulators and private firms around the world. (Library of Congress)

* Another source that you may look into is FORTUNE MAGAZINE. It normally gives background on large industries and their product. Faxing a resume' to any company that matches your "cognitive component" is within accepted industry procedures.

* Consider **CONSULTING.** Contemplate the skills set that can transition from your past or current job experience to the action plan of having a private agency. Whatever field you infiltrate, you will benefit from your experience, knowledge, innovation using your higher level thinking skills with the new integration of technology in the communication processes more than any other projected field you can become a CONSULTANT in your field of competency. **Be the best you can be.**

I WILL transition with this hope for everyone. In every situation and circumstance, portray who you are with definitions of integrity, foresight and a constant pursuit of the extraordinary, always remembering whose shoulders you stood on to rise up **to be the cream that you are! It is all**

good to bring someone up with you. Good citizenship is comprised of compassion and it's a challenge to be executed in all aspects of life. With all the changes in this decade, our fundamental purpose should be the same. To create a world that recognizes the value of every working person who labor with love and a mindset that fosters hopes, aspirations and well-being for today's and future generations.

HEADS-UP FOR NEW MANAGERS AND SUPERVISORS:
It's a well-known fact: "IF risks cannot be eliminated, you should attempt to reduce it to a minimum." You have the right to take charge of implemented policies in regarded to employees performance, behavior, and resulting disciplinary actions. My basic encouragement and unrequested recommendations are gleaned from personal experience and **DO NOT** intend to impinge on or to override any Company Policy or Best Practices that are already in place.

WHAT I will briefly share with you are from my research, observations and some personal experience. My viewpoint is to empower you, as I have extended advice to graduating Students, Professional and Specialists. "**When you decide to succeed at something, you take a whole new attitude and things will begin to happen in your favor.**" One man's mantra, which I fully endorse is: "**My personal mission is to bring all the energy I have to everything I do, every moment of every day, to family, job,** (worship) **and everything in between.**" Jim Latham, Businessman, Florida.

CAREER success is for people who are fully committed, despite the economy or whatever the complexities and the mayhem. They invest highly in mutual job benefits, because strong motivation empowers them to contribute to the company's best interests and their business success. Under your supervision, the workers are the foremost contributors to production and wealth. I know also that the best way to predict the future is to create it. To bring employees in line and try to persuade them in a positive way to do what they ought to do without undue pressure, and to make peace and build bridges. This may be a minor duty, but calls for major commitment if you have diversified population!

MANAGERS are to be progressive, creating a new order of things by "**simply motivate by leading.**" Former President Bill Clinton said, "**There is nothing more difficult to take in hand, more perilous to conduct, or more uncertain in its success than to take the lead in the**

introduction of a new order of things. Because the innovator has for enemies all those who have done well under the old conditions." Various factors can influence your degree of success, Work experience, up-dated knowledge, skills, talents, training, and knowing company policies are itself a prime determinant. "**The desire for knowledge, like the thirst for riches increases even with the acquisition of it**." For instance, I've acquired many college courses and extra-curricular studies outside of my career, some of them I've never utilized in practice. "**It was for me the need to know** - the intelligence that enlightens."

Seriously, Managers, if you have difficulty with motivation for change, look at your goals. "Change is constant." Change can be a refreshing enhancement in today's business environment, recognizing its importance, and the positive effects it can have, plus all the good cumulative benefits relative to employee's productivity, normalcy and the higher level of economic well-being these changes can create for your Company. Recognize that you are creating a lasting and important impression for yourself, employees, and a positive investment in your career and mostly for the Company's notoriety! Meet and beat the challenges and opportunities presented by today's technology changes, by cultivating skilled diverse workforce.

Every day, we encounter things that amaze us, good or bad which causes questions to arise. **Investigate, probe, acknowledge, respond and congratulate. Daily implement these priorities. Life is not without risks. All managers need to collaborate build coalitions, coordinate, and put their egos aside for the good of the organization. Here are some useful nuggets:**

* **Reflexive reactions are often irrational, so utilize the skills of active listening and come up with solutions that create a win-win situation.**
* **The ability to listen, listen, and listen,** without evaluation and premature criticism is particularly appropriate for business managers.
* **Your effectiveness** will depend on how well you can influence the morale of the workers.

* Develop Team intervention techniques for a thorough analyses of cause and effect to resolve an exasperated situation.
* Develop rapport with all cultures and skill-set.
* Don't ignore or fake attention. They'll know.
* Stay on topic to clarify the details you need.
* Give rational response to important questions.
* Find positive outlet to release negative energy.
* Acknowledge, respond, respect differences.
* It's counter-intuitive to label differences as wrong or to be inherently critical because of our own values rather than using complementary and useful alternatives in our evaluations.
* It is said that **"one negative interaction requires five positive ones to neutralize it."**
* When an employee **express a job-related concern,** seek first to understand and be fully cognizant of the problem and deal with it as soon as possible. Hurt feelings can result in conflicts and issues. We will agree that we are engaging a generation who believes in instant response and gratification; thanks to technology.
* **Reengineer and redefine your job to align yourself positively with knowledge of the new advances in communication technologies.**

THIS writer wishes to make it absolutely clear, these are SUGGESTIONS ONLY for new supervisors, not advice to change policies. My goal is to give you a "heads up" to recognize, analyze, assimilate and correct any reported disharmony since **"no one can solve problems that one does not know exist." YOU ARE A CREAM! Good luck for on-the job success! Each day affirm your success and GOD's blessings.**

ABOUT THE AUTHOR

ANTONETH L. WILLIAMS

Before embarking on the wonderful challenge of writing current Knowledge/Experienced base books, Ann has earned degrees and certifications from the University of Hartford, CT, Rollins College of Education, Saint Leo College of Education / Exceptional Education. She has certificates for History and English Literature from the University of London, England, (Overseas Division). **Ann also** has an accumulation of certificates and achievement awards for excellence in Business and Education. **Ann** had written training manuals and monthly newsletters for a Corporation's Home and Field offices, and had also published articles in Business and Industry Magazines. See her current guidebook focusing on "SURVIVING FEEDBACK FRENZIES" - a road map with guidelines for finding jobs and also for defusing nonproductive anomalies in employee relationships in the workplace.